HAMLET

Also in the No Fear Shakespeare Graphic Novels series:

Macbeth
Romeo and Juliet

NO FEAR SHAKESPEARE | Graphic Novels

HAMLET

Illustrated by Neil Babra

SPARKNOTES

Spark Publishing
120 Fifth Avenue
New York, NY 10011
www.sparknotes.com

ISBN-13: 978-1-4114-9873-0
ISBN-10: 1-4114-9873-9

Library of Congress Cataloging-in-Publication Data

Babra, Neil, 1978-
   Hamlet / [Illustrated by Neil Babra].
      p. cm.--(No Fear Shakespeare Graphic Novels)
   Adaptation of Hamlet by William Shakespeare.
   ISBN-13: 978-1-4114-9873-0 (pbk.)
   ISBN-10: 1-4114-9873-9 (pbk.)
   1. Graphic novels. I. Shakespeare, William, 1564-1616. Hamlet. II. Title.
PN6727.B218H36 2008
741.5'973--dc22

                                                              2007061807

Please submit changes or report errors to www.sparknotes.com/errors.

Printed and bound in the United States

20   19   18   17   16   15   14

Acknowledgments

Thanks foremost to my editor, Nina Shen Rastogi, and to Gregory Johnson, Kevin Baier, and Michele Able at SparkNotes. Thanks very much to Binh Danh for his indispensable technical assistance and moral support. Thanks also to Derek Kirk Kim and Hope Larson for their greatly helpful technical advice, and to Scott McCloud, Amy Kim Ganter, Kazu Kibuishi, and the *Flight* crew for their seminal and constant encouragement. Thanks also to Dylan Meconis. And of course, thanks and much love to my family and friends, especially Mom and Dad!

CHARACTERS

HAMLET
The prince of Denmark

CLAUDIUS
The new king of Denmark, Hamlet's uncle

GERTRUDE
The queen of Denmark, Hamlet's mother

HORATIO
Hamlet's friend

POLONIUS
The Lord Chamberlain

OPHELIA
Polonius's daughter

LAERTES

Polonius's son

FORTINBRAS

The prince of Norway, son of King Fortinbras

THE GHOST

A vision of Hamlet's dead father, the former king of Denmark

ROSENCRANTZ and GUILDENSTERN

Hamlet's former schoolmates

OSRIC, VOLTIMAND, and CORNELIUS

Courtiers

FRANCISCO, MARCELLUS, and BARNARDO

Watch guards

ACT ONE

3

4

6

In that fight, our courageous Hamlet killed old King Fortinbras, who--by law--surrendered his territories with his life. If our king had lost, he would have had to do the same.

But now old Fortinbras's bold but unproven young son--also called Fortinbras--has gathered a bunch of hungry thugs to secure the lands his father lost.

As far as I understand, that's why we're posted here tonight and there's such a commotion in Denmark lately.

This must be why the king haunts us now, since he began these wars.

In the high Roman Empire, just before the mighty Julius Caesar fell, corpses rose out of their graves and ran through the streets speaking gibberish.

There were shooting stars, and blood mixed with the morning dew, and threatening signs on the face of the sun.

And now we've had similar omens of terrible things to come, as if heaven and earth have joined together to warn us of our fate.

I-2.

Although the memories of my dear brother Hamlet's death are still fresh and green, life must go on.

Therefore, with sadness and delight do I marry my former sister-in-law--

we shall have joy in our funerals and sorrowful dirges at our wedding. And for your support, I thank you all.

• • •

Now, down to business. As you know, young Fortinbras--underestimating my strength or imagining that the death of the king has thrown my country into turmoil--dreams of an advantage and never stops pestering me with demands that I surrender the territory his father has lost.

So I've written to Fortinbras's uncle, the new king of Norway. He's a bedridden old man who knows nothing of his nephew's plans. I've told him to stop Fortinbras, and I ask you, good Cornelius and Voltemand, to deliver the letter.

We'll do our duty to you in this and everything else.

15

Frailty, thy name is "woman"!

My uncle, despite being my father's brother, resembles him no better than I do Hercules--and yet she married him before she could even break in the shoes she wore to the funeral! A stuipd animal would have mourned its mate longer!

She married less than a month after my father died--her cheeks didn't even have time to dry! How wickedly she sped to that incestuous bed! This cannot come to any good...

Break, my heart-- for my tongue cannot speak of this.

Hello my lord!

Horatio?

The same--

Ever your humble servant.

No, sir, my friend.

25

27

29

30

33

34

39

40

ACT TWO

47

*arras = tapestry

*A Biblical character who unwittingly promised to sacrifice his own daughter
**Lyrics from a popular song

But I, and those with better judgment than I, found it excellent-- well ordered and clever, but still restrained.

One critic noted that it used no vulgar language to spice up the dialogue, and no showy turns of phrase to call attention to the playwright.

NOD

He called it an honest play.

I loved one speech in particular--the part about Pyrrhus murdering Priam in the Trojan War.*

Let me see, how did it go--

"The savage Pyrrhus, with armor as black as his intentions,"

"Now he has dressed himself from head to toe in red,"

"lay like the night inside the Trojan Horse."

"smeared with the blood of the enemy's fathers, mothers, daughters, and sons."

"His eyes glowing like rubies, the hellish Pyrrhus seeks old king Priam."

So, you can proceed.

*From the Roman epic The Aeneid

68

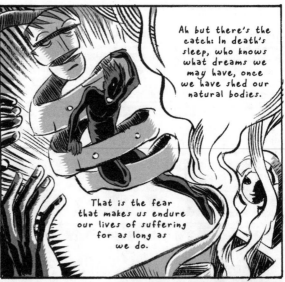

Ah but there's the catch: In death's sleep, who knows what dreams we may have, once we have shed our natural bodies.

That is the fear that makes us endure our lives of suffering for as long as we do.

To die is to sleep--

No more.

A sleep that ends the heartache and natural shocks that are inherited by all living flesh.

To die, to sleep-- perhaps to dream!

After all, who would put up with life's humiliations-- the abuse from superiors, the insults of arrogant men, the pangs of unrequited love, the law's inefficiency, the rudeness of those in office, the mistreatment of good people by the wicked--

when you could simply take your knife out and quit.

Who would choose to grunt and sweat through an exhausting life unless he was afraid of something dreadful after death-- the undiscovered country from which no visitor ever returns, the mystery that makes us bear the evils we know rather than rush off to seek the ones we don't?

Fear of death makes us all cowards, and our natural boldness becomes weak with too much thinking. Actions that should be carried out at once get misdirected and stop being actions at all.

*nunnery = both "convent" and "brothel"

93

*nothing = in Shakespeare's time, slang for female genitalia

103

By God, it is indeed like a camel.

To me it looks like a weasel.

It does have a back like a weasel's.

Or like a whale.

Very like a whale.

I will come to my mother soon.

They'll go along with me no matter how mad I act...

I will say so to her.

Leave me, "friends."

You wretched, rash, intruding fool, farewell. I mistook you for your superior. You got what was coming to you! You found out that it's dangerous to be so pesky, didn't you?

Quit wringing your hands! Stop! Sit yourself down, and let me wring your heart, for I shall, if it's still soft enough--if your damned habits haven't hardened it so that it can't feel anything at all.

What have I done that you dare to wag your tongue so rudely against me!

Such an act that ruins modesty, turns virtue into hypocrisy, replaces the rose on the fair forehead of innocent love with a blister, makes marriage vows as false as gamblers' oaths--oh, such a deed that plucks the very soul from the body of marriage and turns sweet religion into meaningless blather.

Heaven looks down on this earth with an angry face, as if it were dooms-day, and is sickened by the thought of your act.

What act have I committed that thunders so loudly before it's revealed?

Look here upon this picture, and upon this one too, these paintings of two brothers.

*Zeus = king of the gods; Mars = god of war; Mercury = messenger of the gods

If wickedness can overtake even an old woman's bones, then let it melt mine like wax.

Declare it to the world! It's no longer a shame to act on impulsive passion, now that the old are doing so, and reason has become a servant to desire!

Oh Hamlet, speak no more! You make me see into my very soul, and there I see spots so black and ingrained that they can never be cleaned away.

Yes, and you lie in the sweaty stench of your dirty sheets, wet with corruption, honeying and making love in this animal **filth**.

Oh, speak to me no more! These words are like **daggers**! No more, sweet Hamlet.

A **murderer** and a **villain**, a wretched **slave** who's not worth a twentieth of a **tenth** of my lordly father-- the **worst** of kings, a **thief** of the empire and the throne, who **stole** the precious crown and put it in his pocket--

--a ragged, clownish king--

No more!

ACT FOUR

135

IV-5.

I will not speak with her.

She's insistent. In fact, she's crazed. You cannot help but pity her.

What does she want?

She speaks much of her father, says she hears conspiracies everywhere, coughs, beats her breast, rages at nothing, and babbles nonsense.

It would be a good idea to speak with her, since she might lead those with evil intentions to dangerous conclusions...

NOD

K-CHAK

Where is the beautiful majesty of Denmark?

What are you doing, Ophelia?

142

Now that he's returned, Hamlet will surely learn that you are here as well. You are both known to be excellent fencers--we'll organize a duel and set bets on you both.

I'll do it.

I bought some oil from a hawker, so deadly that if you dip a knife in it, no medicine in the world can save the man scratched with it.

Hamlet is so careless, high-minded, and naive that he won't inspect the swords. You can easily trick him and select a sword with a sharpened point so that you may avenge your father with a single thrust.

I'll dab my sword with the stuff so that even a touch will mean death for Hamlet.

But if this plan should fail or our intentions are discovered, it would be better if we'd never tried it. We need a backup plan. Let me see...

I have it! When you are both hot and thirsty--which you will be because you'll fight violently to ensure it-- Hamlet will call for a drink.

I'll have a cup ready. If by chance he escapes being stuck by your poisoned sword, this drink will kill him.

But it was not long before her garments, heavy with water, pulled the poor wretched girl from her song...

to a muddy death.

Then she is drowned.

Drowned, drowned!

You've had too much water already, poor Ophelia, so I'll hold back my tears.

And yet, to cry is in our nature, and Nature will not be swayed, even by shame.

Farewell, my lord. I'd make a fiery speech, but...

Sob

Let's follow, Gertrude. I had to do so much to calm his rage! Now I fear this will get him started again. So let's follow.

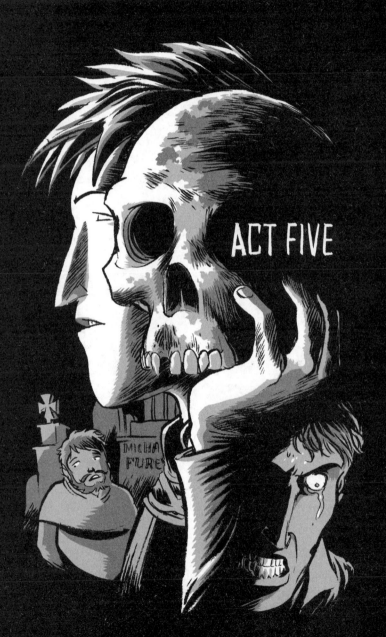

ACT FIVE

170

About the Artist

Neil Babra grew up in western Pennsylvania and now resides in the San Francisco Bay Area. He is a regular contributor to, and now assistant editor of, the Harvey Award-winning comics anthology *Flight* from Random House Books. He has also contributed short comics and cartoons to various other collections, including *You Ain't No Dancer* and *Nickelodeon* magazine. This is his first book-length comics work. You can see more of his work at www.neilcomics.com.

"Shakespeare, Shakespeare, Shakespeare"

An Introduction to Shakespeare's Life, World & Plays
(IN PLAIN ENGLISH)

NO FEAR
SHAKESPEARE™
A Companion

* **Everything you need to know** about the man, his work, and his world.

$9.95

No Fear Shakespeare: A Companion
ISBN-13: 978-1-4114-9746-7   ISBN-10: 1-4114-9746-5